THEMATIC UNIT

SELF-ESTEEM

Written by Diane Williams

Illustrated by Blanqui Apodaca and Paula Spence

Teacher Created Materials, Inc.
P.O. Box 1040
Huntington Beach, CA 92647
©1990 Teacher Created Materials, Inc.
Made in U.S.A.

ISBN 1-55734-269-5

Table of Contents

Introduction

Self-Esteem contains a captivating whole language, thematic unit which will help children build positive self-concepts. Its 80 exciting pages are filled with a wide variety of lesson ideas and reproducible pages designed for use with early primary children. At its core is a high-quality children's literature selection, *George and Martha*. For the stories in this book, activities are included which set the stage for reading, encourage the enjoyment of the book, and extend the concepts gained. In addition, the theme is connected to the curriculum with activities in language arts, math, science, social studies, art, music, and life skills (cooking, physical education, etc.) Many of these activities encourage cooperative learning. Suggestions and patterns for bulletin boards and unit management tools are additional time savers for the busy teacher. Futhermore, directions for student-created Big Books and a culminating activity, which allow students to synthesize their knowledge in order to produce products that can be shared beyond the classroom, highlight this very complete teacher resource.

This thematic unit includes:

☐ **a literature selection** — a summary of a children's book with related lessons (complete with reproducible pages) that cross the curriculum

☐ **poetry** — suggested selections and lessons enabling students to write and publish their own works

☐ **planning guides** — suggestions for sequencing lessons each day of the unit

☐ **language experience ideas** — daily suggestions as well as activities across the curriculum, including Big Books

☐ **bulletin board ideas** — suggestions and plans for student-created and/or interactive bulletin boards

☐ **homework suggestions** — extending the unit to the child's home

☐ **curriculum connections** — in language arts, math, science, social studies, art, music, and life skills such as cooking and physical education

☐ **group projects** — to foster cooperative learning

☐ **a culminating activity** — which requires students to synthesize their learning to produce a product or engage in an activity that can be shared with others

☐ **a bibliography** — suggesting additional books on the theme

---

To keep this valuable resource intact so that it can be used year after year, you may wish to punch holes in the pages and store them in a three-ring binder.

Introduction (cont.)

WHY WHOLE LANGUAGE?

A whole language approach involves children in using all modes of communication: reading, writing, listening, speaking, observing, illustrating, experiencing, and doing. Communication skills are interconnected and integrated into lessons that emphasize the whole of language rather than isolating its parts. The lessons revolve around selected literature. Reading is not taught as a separate subject from writing and spelling, for example. A child reads, writes (spelling appropriately for his/her level), speaks, listens, etc. in response to a literature experience introduced by the teacher. In this way, language skills grow naturally, stimulated by involvement and interest in the topic at hand.

WHY THEMATIC PLANNING?

One very useful tool for implementing an integrated whole language program is thematic planning. By choosing a theme with correlating literature selections for a unit of study, a teacher can plan activities throughout the day that lead to a cohesive, in-depth study of the topic. Students will be practicing and applying their skills in meaningful contexts. Consequently, they will tend to learn and retain more. Both teachers and students will be freed from a day that is broken into unrelated segments of isolated drill and practice.

WHY COOPERATIVE LEARNING?

Besides academic skills and content, students need to learn social skills. No longer can this area of development be taken for granted. Students must learn to work cooperatively in groups in order to function well in modern society. Group activities should be a regular part of school life and teachers should consciously include social objectives as well as academic objectives in their planning. For example, a group working together to write a report may need to select a leader. The teacher should make clear to the students and monitor the qualities of good leader-follower group interaction just as he/she would state and monitor the academic goals of the project.

WHY BIG BOOKS?

An excellent cooperative, whole language activity is the production of Big Books. Groups of students, or the whole class, can apply their language skills, content knowledge, and creativity to produce a Big Book that can become a part of the classroom library to be read and reread. These books make excellent culminating projects for sharing beyond the classroom with parents, librarians, other classes, etc. Big Books can be produced in many ways and this thematic unit book includes directions for at least one method you may choose.

George and Martha

by James Marshall

George and Martha is a set of five short stories about two hippopotamuses who are the best of friends. The stories are delightful. They are great for creative drama and puppetry because they are simple and funny. In addition, the stories are ideal material for the discussion of self–esteem because they examine feelings, self–concept, and the value of friends.

Story 1–"Split Pea Soup"

Martha makes split pea soup for George, not realizing that he hates it. George doesn't want to hurt Martha's feelings, so he eats as much as he can. Finally, in desperation, he hides some soup in his slippers! Martha sees this, and the two friends discuss the problem. Then Martha makes George chocolate chip cookies.

The outline below is a suggested plan for using the various activities that are presented in this unit. You should adapt these ideas to fit your own classroom situation.

Sample Plan

Day I

- Read poem "The Meal" (see page 41)
- Discuss and chart "Foods I Hate to Eat, Foods I Love to Eat"
- Play "This Little Piggy Ate..." (page 8)
- Introduce *George and Martha*
- Read Story 1, "Split Pea Soup"
- Activity Centers
  Book Corner (page 6)
  Let's Play With Peas (page 8)
- "Word Hunt" worksheet (page 9)
- Retell story with props(see pages 46-49)
- Make puppets (pages 64-65)

Day II

- Play "This Little Piggy Ate..."again (page 8)
- Make collage,"Foods I Love and Hate to Eat" (page 7)
- Reread story
- Activity Centers
  Book Corner
  Let's Play With Peas
  Retell the Story
- Learn and sing "Eat It Up" or "Brussel Sprouts"
- Discuss "Let's Cook" rules
- Make and taste split pea soup (page 69)

- Read poem "Turtle Soup" (see page 41)
- Create a puppet play of story
- "Fill the Cookie" worksheet (page 10)

Day III

- Share collages
- Play "This Little Piggy Ate..." with "chocolate chip cookies" for the last line (page 8)
- Reread story. Have children supply key words "split pea soup" and "chocolate chip cookies"
- Review "Let's Cook" rules (page 68)
- Bake cookies (page 69)
- Read poem "Crunch and Lick" (see page 41)
- Graph number of chips in cookies (page 7), then eat.
- Activity Centers
  Book Corner
  Let's Play With Peas
  Retell the Story
  Puppet Plays
- Sing "Biscuits in the Oven"
- Share puppet plays
- "I Can Add" worksheet (page 11)
- Homework: "I Am Growing!"(page 14)

Overview of Activities

SETTING THE STAGE

1. Set up a book corner. Make it a comfortable place to be. Collect books related to *George and Martha* (see Bibliography, page 80, for suggestions). Provide time for the children to look at and read these books on their own. Adult volunteers or older students may help those who cannot read yet, but all children will enjoy the pictures.

2. Have the Activity Center, "Let's Play with Peas," ready to go. Complete directions are on page 8.

3. Prepare Story Retelling Props (pages 47-49) after choosing the Story Retelling Activity you will use for the unit from page 46.

4. Share appropriate poetry. (See page 41 for suggestions.)

5. Conduct a discussion about foods that are liked and foods not liked. Chart the children's answers. Remember, even if young children cannot read what is written, they gain valuable language skills and self-esteem when they see that their own words can be written down.

Foods I Like	Foods I Don't Like
Tommy - Pizza Mary Ellen - Ice Cream Paula - Peas	Suzi - Brussels Sprouts Eddie - Eggplant

6. Play the chant game "This Little Piggy Ate..." Directions are on page 8.

7. Introduce the characters George and Martha by using a set of figures from the Story Retelling Props (pages 47-49). These can be prepared for use on a flannel board, magnetic board, or as stick puppets. Let the children know that George and Martha are hippos who are good friends.

8. Show the book cover. Tell the children that the book has five short stories in it. The first one is called "Split Pea Soup." Ask them to guess what the story will be about.

ENJOYING THE STORY

1. Read "Split Pea Soup" for enjoyment. Encourage the children to guess what will happen next after you complete each page. As you read the story ask the following questions to focus on the concepts of Martha's feelings and the value of friendship.

    1. *Why did George eat the split pea soup?*
    2. *Would you eat it if your friend made you split pea soup?*
    3. *What problem did George have?*
    4. *Why did George pour the soup into his slippers?*
    5. *How would you feel if your friend did that to you?*
    6. *What do you think George should have done?*
    7. *Have you ever hidden food you didn't want to eat? Why?*
    8. *Why did Martha make chocolate chip cookies?*

2. Use the Story Retelling Props to retell the story.

3. Make George and Martha paper bag puppets. (Patterns and directions on pages 64 and 65.)

4. Make puppet plays of the story. (See page 45 for suggestions.)

Overview of Activities *(cont.)*

EXTENDING THE STORY

1. Make collages of "Foods I Hate" and "Foods I Love." Fold 12" x 18" construction paper in half for each child. Have them draw a small happy face on one side and a sad face on the other. Then have them draw appropriate food pictures or cut them out of magazines and glue to the paper.

2. Cook pea soup. Directions and recipe are on pages 68 and 69.

3. Learn and sing "Eat It Up" and/or "Brussel Sprouts," (see Bibliography for source).

4. Poetry–See page 41 for suggestions.

5. Have a Tasting Party! Make it an occasion by having the children make placemats, set a fancy table, and discuss table manners. (The poem "Table Manners" is a good starter; see page 41 for source.)

6. Do initial consonant activity sheet "Fill The Cookie" (page 10).

7. Bake chocolate chip cookies. (See pages 68 and 69 for directions and recipe.)

8. Before eating, count chocolate chips in the cookies baked. Graph the counts. An easy way to do this is to give each child a piece of sticky notepaper on which to record his count. Then have him/her attach it to the appropriate section of a chart as shown.

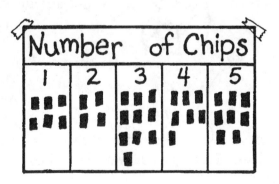

9. Use "I Can Add" activity sheet (page 11).

Activities for "Split Pea Soup"

Let's Play With Peas!

Tub of Peas

Materials: Plastic tub, funnel, measuring cups and spoons, various sizes of containers, several packages of dried peas (try beans later if you like)

Teacher Preparation:

Spread out a plastic tablecloth or old shower curtain on the floor. Place a table on it to hold the materials. For simple clean up, move table to the side; lift up the plastic sheet by the corners; pour spilled peas back into the tub.

Directions For The Children:

Play with the peas! Practice measuring.

Pea Playdough

Materials: Playdough, dried peas

Teacher Preparation:
Mix some dried peas into the playdough.
This gives the children a new tactile experience.
Put the playdough on the table beside the tub of peas.

Directions For The children: Free play.

"This Little Piggy Ate..." Chant Game

Use a variation of the nursery rhyme, "This Little Pig Went to Market," to teach a language pattern and continue the discussion of foods that are liked and disliked.
Prepare sentence strips for a pocket chart, flannel board, or magnetic board of the chant below.

This little piggy ate_____
This little piggy ate_____
This little piggy ate_____
This little piggy ate_____
And this little piggy said,
"I want_____   "

Use the "Foods I Like and Don't Like" chart to pick unliked foods for the first four blanks and a liked food for the last blank. Put appropriate word cards into the pocket chart and have children chant.
Variations:
Have children take off their shoes and socks. Seat them in a circle on the floor. As the rhyme is chanted, children wiggle their toes as in the original Mother Goose version. Go around the circle to have children take turns giving the missing words. The word "piggy" may be changed to "hippo" and "chocolate chip cookies" may be included in the last line.

Name______________________________________

Word Hunt!

Find the word George.

Draw a red circle around it.

Find the word Martha.

Draw a blue circle around it.

Red	*ME*	**stop**
go	**up**	*Martha*
Me	*Go*	**go**
MARTHA	**Dad**	**George**
Mom	*No*	**red**
George	**GEORGE**	*no*
Name		**MARTHA**

Fill the Cookie!

1. Cut out the pictures that start with **Cc.**

2. Paste them on the cookie.

I Can Add!

1. Count the chocolate chips.   3. Add.

2. Print the number under the cookie.   4. Color.

_____ + _____ = ☐

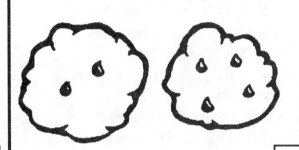

_____ + _____ = ☐

_____ + _____ = ☐

_____ + _____ = ☐

_____ + _____ = ☐

_____ + _____ = ☐

Story 2–"The Flying Machine"

Summary

George is determined to be the first hippopotamus to fly. He climbs into a hot air balloon basket. But he goes nowhere. Martha suggests he might be too heavy, so George climbs out. Away flies his machine! Then Martha cheers him up.

Sample Plan

Day I	Day II
• Share Homework Sheet (page 14)	• Ask a child to retell story using story props or puppets
• Discuss Measuring Activities	• Learn song "I Can Fly!"
• "I Am Growing" Graph	• Imagine flying up, up, up
• Activity Centers (keep the previous centers set up)	• "Up Up Up" worksheet, (page 20)
• Measuring Corner (page 12)	• Share worksheet
• "How Big Am I?" worksheet (page 16)	• Activity Centers
• Read "The Flying Machine"	• Science - "Make a Parachute!" (page 53), "Make A Twirly!" (page 54), and/or "Make George Go Up" (page 55)
• Homework-"How Heavy Am I?" worksheet (page 17)	• Gym Activity - Experiment with parachute
• Weigh and measure children	• Share songs and plays
• Retell story using story props (pages 46-49)	• Homework - Ask children to bring tub toys
• Sing songs (see page 13 for suggestions)	• "Fill the Balloon" worksheet (page 21)
• Prepare a puppet play	

Overview of Activities

SETTING THE STAGE

1. Set up a Measuring Activity Center. See page 15 for directions. Do not dismantle the "Peas" Center, for it is also a type of "measuring" center and a discussion of types of measures–volume, linear, weight–can be enhanced by the concrete activities in the two centers.

2. Gather the children into a circle to share their "I Am Growing!" homework sheets. Have them tell how they got the size of their baby foot. Find out what they think about the change in their foot size.

3. Weigh and measure the children. You may wish to use a parent volunteer or the school nurse as an assistant. Help each child fill in the appropriate blanks on the worksheets, "How Big Am I?" (question 1) and "How Heavy Am I?" (question 2). "How Heavy Am I?" should be kept to be returned to the children as a homework assignment. "How Big Am I?" may be completed independently by the children following the next activity and using the measuring tools in the Measuring Activity Center.

4. Make an "I Am Growing Taller!" graph (directions on page 15) for the children in your class.

5. Poetry–See page 41 for suggestions.

Overview of Activities *(cont.)*

ENJOYING THE STORY

1. Read "The Flying Machine" aloud to the class for enjoyment.

2. Discuss self-esteem concepts–George's need to be noticed and respected. Then focus on the concept of embarrassment and how it can affect self-esteem by discussing the following questions:

   Why did George want to be the first hippo to fly?

   Why did George climb out of the flying machine?

   What could he have done instead?

   Why did the flying machine fly away?

   How did George feel then?

   What did Martha do to make him feel better?

   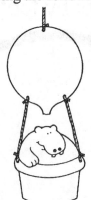

3. Story Retelling Activity (see page 46).

4. Make "George's Flying Machine." Patterns and directions are on pages 18-19. Show pictures of hot air balloons so students can see how colorful they are. Hang finished projects from the ceiling.

5. Make puppet plays of the story. Use George and Martha paper bag puppets from the first story.

6. Poetry–See page 41 for suggestions.

EXTENDING THE STORY

1. Write a class story about what you would see from the air. Record responses as children dictate. Read aloud together.

2. Use the "Up Up Up" activity sheet (page 20). Depending on the abilities of your students, you may have them draw, draw and label, or write their responses to the question on the paper. Let students share their products with the group. Being the center of attention is a great self-esteem builder!

3. Use "Make A Parachute" (page 53), "Make A Twirly" (page 54), and/or "Make George Go Up" (page 55). These activities may be done on separate days so the children can explore various types of "flight."

4. Learn songs "I Must Be Growing," "I Can Fly," "Growing Up," and "I Wonder If I'm Growing" (see Bibliography, page 80, for sources).

5. Do initial consonant activity sheet "Fill The Balloon" (page 21).

6. If your school is lucky enough to have a real parachute in its collection of physical education equipment, share it with the children. One fun activity is to position the class evenly spaced around the edge of the parachute which has been spread open on the gym floor or school yard. Children bend over, grasp the edge with both hands, and, on the count of three, raise their arms into the air. The parachute will billow on an air cushion. Practice working together to make lovely billows, ripples, and waves.

Name _____

I Am Growing!

1.   Trace your shoe in the footprint. Someone may help you.

2.   Ask an adult to help you know the size of your baby foot.

3.   Draw your baby foot inside your big foot.

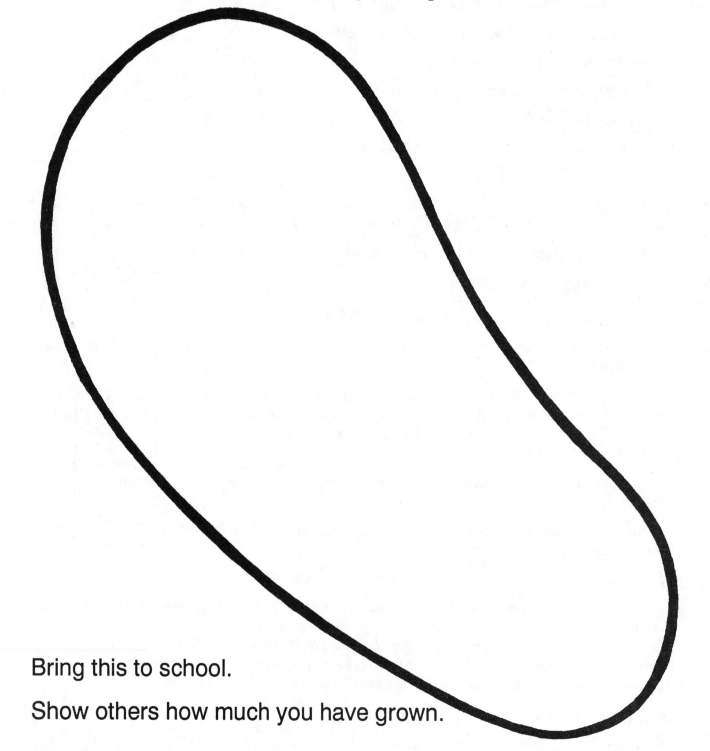

Bring this to school.

Show others how much you have grown.

Measuring

Measures are not easy for children to grasp as abstractions. A good way to start measuring with young children is to play with measuring, focusing on "Me Measures."

Set Up a Measuring Corner

Include several tape measures, yardsticks, rulers, nurse's scale, a balance scale, a bathroom scale, and some objects to weigh.

Make an "I Am Growing" Graph

Materials: Large chart or butcher paper, string, scissors, tape

Teacher Preparation:

Make a chart as in the diagram.

Directions:

Take a small group of children at a time.

Measure the height of each child. Cut a piece of string his height.

Tape the string vertically on the chart.

Ask the child to print his name under it.

Mark the date and his current height above it.

Cut another piece of string his height for him to take home.

Do this activity again later in the year, and compare heights.

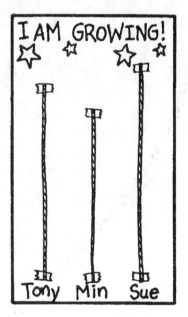

Practice Weighing Things

Discuss:

What things are weighed? Why?

How can you tell which of two things is heavier?

Weigh each child. If necessary, do this privately and be discreet.

Give the children a wide variety of objects to weigh.

Name _____

How Big Am I?

1. I am _____ tall.

2. I am taller than _____.

3. I am shorter than _____.

4. My foot is _____ long.

5. My hand is _____ long.

Trace 4 fingers.

Find your longest finger. Color it red.
Find your shortest finger. Color it yellow.
Measure your fingers. Write how long they are.

Name_____   *"The Flying Machine"*

How Heavy Am I?

When I was born, I weighed _____ .

Now I weigh _____ .

I weigh more than _____ .

Draw things that are heavier than you are. Name them.

George's Flying Machine

Color.

Cut out.

Punch out each ◯.

Thread a long string through each ◯.

Print your name on the back.

Name_____ *"The Flying Machine"*

George's Flying Machine (cont.)

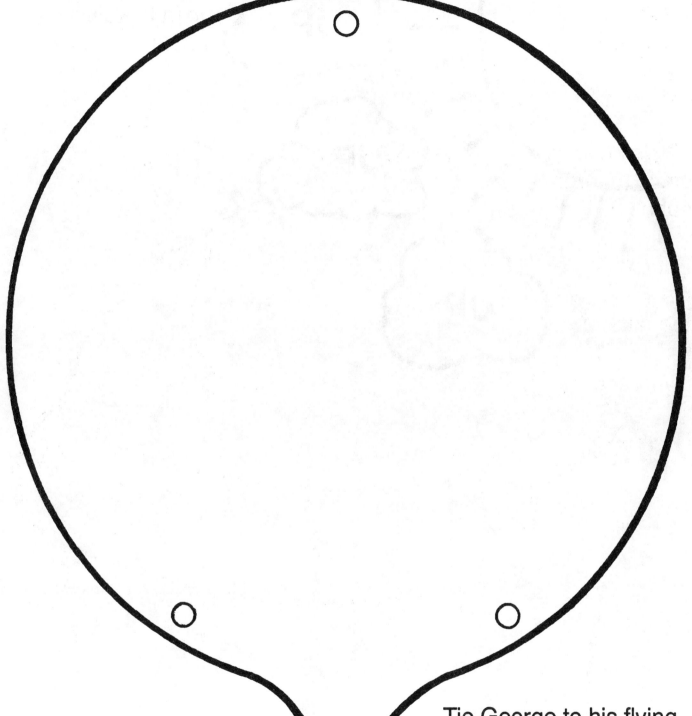

Color bright colors.
Cut out.
Punch out each ◯.

Tie George to his flying machine.
Thread a string through the top.
Hang George up!

Imagine you flew
up in the air. What
would you see?

Fill the Balloon!

1. Cut out the pictures that start with **Bb**.

2. Paste them in the balloon.

Story 3 – "The Tub"

Summary

George likes to peek in windows. Accidentally, he peeks in on Martha when she is having a bath. She is furious and teaches him a lesson.

Sample Plan

Day I	Day II
• Sort and classify Tub Toys (page 22)	• Play tub toy memory (page 23)
• Play Pass the Tub Toys (page 22)	• Reread "The Tub"
• Share bathtime poems (see page 41)	• Dramatize story
• Discuss why we bathe and tub safety	• Learn poem "Blowing Bubbles" (see page 41)
• Use "Safe for the Tub" (page 25)	• "Let's Play with Bubbles" (page 56)
• Read "The Tub"	• Use "Match the Bubbles" (page 26)
• Discuss privacy and respect	• Sing "Crowded Tub" or "Rubber Ducky"
• Retell story	• Soap painting of tub toy (page 23)
• Use Water Play Center (page 24)	
• Phonics "Fill the Tub" (page 27)	

Overview of Activities

SETTING THE STAGE

1. Sort and classify the tub toys children have brought. Use several variables: color, size, type of toy, shape, etc.

2. Play "Pass the Tub Toys"

   Stand in a circle.
   Pass a tub toy to the right.
   When it is half-way, pass another toy.
   See how many toys can be passed.
   If a toy is dropped, pick it up and pass it.
   If the toys pile up in one place, stop.
   If too many toys are being dropped, stop.
   Collect the toys and start again.
   Pass to the left this time.

3. Set up Activity Center, "Let's Play With Water." See page 24 for directions.

4. Share some or all of the bathtime poems mentioned on page 41.

5. Talk about why we bathe. Relate this to self-esteem by helping children understand that bathing is related to health and good grooming and the better we feel and look, the better we feel about ourselves. Bathing is a task that many children of this age are beginning to do for themselves. Discuss how grown-up it feels to be able to take care of oneself.

6. Discuss bathtime safety. Emphasize no sharp or electrical items.

7. Do "Safe for the Tub" activity sheet (page 25).

Overview of Activities *(cont.)*

ENJOYING THE STORY

1. Read "The Tub" for enjoyment.

2. Discuss self-esteem concepts—the need for privacy and respect.

   Focus on Martha's feelings and the need for privacy.

   > *1. Why do you think George liked peeking in windows?*
   >
   > *2. Do you think he should do this?*
   >
   > *3. Do you think George meant to bother Martha?*
   >
   > *4. Why was Martha so angry?*
   >
   > *5. Why do people need privacy?*
   >
   > *6. Can you make up a new ending?*

3. Story Retelling Activity. (For suggestions see page 46.)

4. Make puppet plays of the story. (For suggestions see page 45.)

EXTENDING THE STORY

1. Play "Memory."

   > Put some tub toys on a tray.
   > Give the children 15 seconds to study the items.
   > Ask them to close their eyes.
   > Remove 1 toy.
   > "What is missing?"

2. Learn the poem, "Blowing Bubbles," (see page 41 for source) to chant while doing science activity below.

3. Set up activity center "Let's Play With Bubbles." See page 56 for directions.

4. Learn the song "Crowded Tub." (See Bibliography, page 80, for source.)

5. Use the following activity sheets:

   "Match the Bubbles" (page 26) and "Fill The Tub" (page 27).

6. Make a soap painting of a tub toy. Mix about 1/2 cup of white laundry soap flakes to each cup of tempera to form a thick paint (like pancake batter). Paint a picture of a tub toy.

Let's Play With Water!

Tub of Toys

Materials:
> Plastic tub
> Plastic sheet
> Newspapers
> Water
> Various tub toys

Teacher Preparation:
> Spread the plastic sheet on the tabletop.
> Spread newspapers on the floor to cut down on slipperiness.
> Ask the children to bring their favorite bathtub toy to school.

Directions For The Children:
> Free Play.
> Sort and classify the toys.
> Tell how you did it.

Tub of Stuff

Materials:
> Plastic tub
> Plastic sheet
> Newspapers
> Water
> Collection of objects -- cork, rock, pencil, sponge, stick, eraser, piece of wax paper, piece of foil, etc.

Teacher Preparation:
> Spread out the plastic sheet on the tabletop.
> Spread old newspapers on the floor to cut down on slipperiness.
> Put the objects out in a plastic container.

Directions For The Children:
> Free Play.
> Find out what floats and what does not float.
> Think about why some things float and other things don't.
> Sort the stuff into two piles -- things that float and things that don't float.
> Experiment with other objects.

Safe for the Tub

1.   Color the objects that are good to take in the tub.

2.   Cross out the ones that are not safe for the tub.

Match the Bubbles

1. Cut out the little bubbles at the bottom of the page.

2. Paste each little bubble beside the correct big bubble.

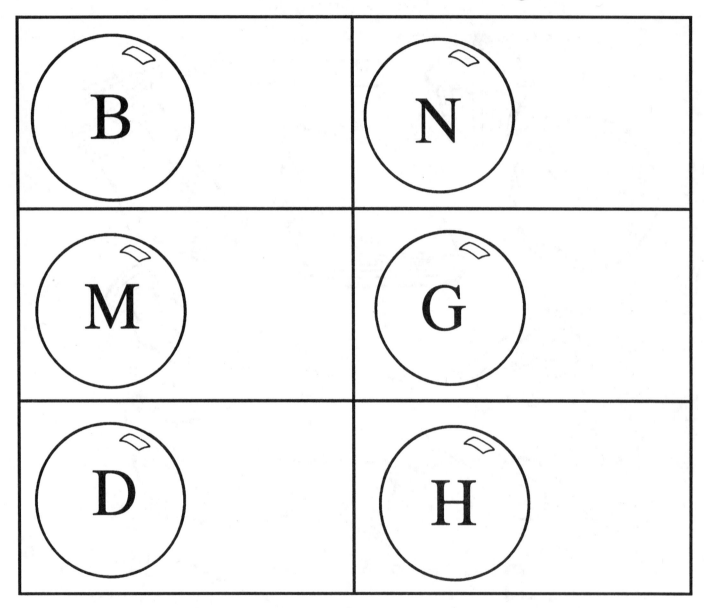

26

Fill the Tub!

Cut out the pictures that start with **Tt.**

Paste them in the tub.

Story 4 – "The Mirror"
Summary

Martha loves to look at herself in the mirror. Finally George gets tired of it. He makes a silly picture of her and pastes it on her mirror. Martha gets quite a scare, but she stops being so vain.

Sample Plan

Day I

- Poem, "Robert, Who Is Often a Stranger to Himself" (see page 41)
- Children study selves in full-length mirror
- Draw self-portraits
- Free play at Activity Center – "Let's Play with Mirrors" (page 30)
- Play "Copy My Face" and "Copy Me" (page 28)
- Read and discuss "The Mirror"
- Do sequence activity sheet (page 31)
- Use "Mirror Fun" activity sheet (page 32)
- Assign homework - Bring reflecting objects (see page 29)

Day II

- Display and share funny reflecting objects
- Reread story
- Retelling the story activity (page 46)
- Dramatize the story (pages 29 and 45)
- Draw "silly" self-portraits
- Use "Magic Mirrors" activity sheet (page 33)
- Make living graphs (pages 29 and 52)
- Do "Fill the Mirror!" activity sheet (page 34)
- Free play at Mirror Activity Center

Overview of Activities
SETTING THE STAGE

1. Read and discuss the poem, "Robert Who Is Often a Stranger to Himself." See page 41 for source.

2. Draw self-portraits. Have children study themselves in a full-length mirror first. The Body Pictures described on page 63 may be used for this activity. Or, large sheets of construction paper may be used for drawings.

3. Set up an Activity Center with a collection of mirrors. See page 30 for directions. Let children have free play with the mirrors before introducing the activities.

4. Play "Copy My Face" and "Copy Me!"

Copy My Face!
Choose a partner.
Stand in front of a big mirror.
One person makes a face.
The partner tries to copy it.
Trade places.

Copy Me!
Choose a partner.
One child pretends to be a mirror.
He mimics the other child's whole body actions.
Trade places.

28

Overview of Activities *(cont.)*

ENJOYING THE STORY

1. Read ''The Mirror'' for enjoyment. Encourage the children to guess what will happen next.

2. Discuss self–esteem concepts. Focus on the concepts of being proud of yourself and how this is different from being vain, conceited or boastful.

> *1. Why does Martha love to look at herself in the mirror?*
>
> *2. Do you like to look at yourself in the mirror sometimes?*
>
> *3. Why did George get tired of Martha looking at herself?*
>
> *4. What did he do?*
>
> *5. Do you think he should have done this?*
>
> *6. Make up a new ending for the story.*

3. Make a sequence story (page 31). Have students color, cut on the lines, and sequence the pictures. They should be glued in order to construction paper. Students who are capable of doing so should be encouraged to write a sentence about each picture. They now have a prop to retell the story at school and home.

4. Use a retelling activity from page 46.

5. Use puppets or child actors to dramatize the story. Use real mirrors. Have children make the ''silly picture'' to put on the mirror.

EXTENDING THE STORY

1. Assign "Funny Reflections" homework. Ask children to look at home, especially in the kitchen, for objects in which they can see their reflections. Bring them to school. Set up display of strangely reflecting objects like shiny spoons, tea kettles, aluminum foil, etc. Let the children experiment with their "funny" reflections.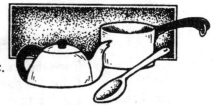

2. Have children draw ''silly'' pictures of themselves as George did of Martha. Be sure to let them share these.

3. Use the worksheets, ''Mirror Fun'' (page 32) and ''Magic Mirrors'' (page 33). Directions for using these pages are on page 30.

4. Make Living Graphs of hair and eye color. See page 52 for directions for this exciting math activity.

5. Do initial consonant activity sheet ''Fill The Mirror'' (page 34).

Let's Play With Mirrors

Set up a Mirror Activity Center

Materials:

Collection of mirrors – various sizes
2 full-size mirrors

Challenges For The Children:

Can you see behind your back?
Can you see over your head?
Look in the mirror to see what is on the ceiling.
Explore old magazine photographs with your mirror.
Print your name. Then look at it with a mirror.

Mirror Fun

Materials:

Several pocket size mirrors

Teacher Preparation:

Ask the children to bring mirrors from home, if possible.
Give each child a copy of "Mirror Fun" (page 32).

Directions For The Children:

Play freely with the mirrors and pictures.
Try to put the edge of your mirror on the picture in a special way so you can still see the whole picture.
Move the mirror a little bit. See what happens.

Magic Mirrors

Materials:

2 identical pocket size mirrors without frames
tape
letter cards

Teacher Preparation:

Tape the 2 mirrors together on one edge, making a hinge.
Copy the page "Magic Mirrors" (page 33) onto tagboard.
Cut out to make letter cards.

Directions For The Children:

Explore the letter cards with the magic mirror.

Exploring Symmetry

As children do the activities above, guide them to an understanding of symmetry which occurs when opposite parts of an object correspond in size, shape, and position. Help them see that this balance can sometimes be in one direction, but not another; e.g., an "A" is symmetrical right to left, but not top to bottom. Symmetrical paintings can be made by having children fold construction paper in half; open it; drip paint onto one half; refold; and open to see the same design on each side.

Sequence Story

*Teacher: See page 29 for directions.

Name_____

Mirror Fun
*See suggested activities, page 30.

Magic Mirrors
See suggested activities, page 30.

				A
B	C	D	E	F
G	H	I	J	K
L	M	N	O	P
Q	R	S	T	U
V	W	X	Y	Z

Fill the Mirror!

1. Cut out the pictures that start with **Mm.**

2. Paste them in Martha's mirror.

Story 5–"The Tooth"
Summary

George is roller skating. He trips and breaks off his right front tooth. George is upset so Martha soothes him. The dentist makes him a gold false tooth. Martha compliments him kindly.

Sample Plan

Day I

- Display and discuss tooth care materials
- Dental care worker visit
- Language experience story
- Care of teeth drawing or story
- "Good or Bad for Teeth" activity sheet (page 37)
- Living Graph (pages 35 and 52)
- Read "The Tooth" aloud
- Sing "Brush Your Teeth"

Day II

- Reread the story
- Do a story retelling activity (page 46)
- Make TV movie (page 36)

- Dramatize "The Tooth"
- Write or tell about a hurt experience
- Study real hippos
- Do "Hippo Puzzle" math activity (pages 50 - 51)
- Do "Fill the Hat" activity sheet (page 39)

Day III

- Culminate George and Martha with a Friendship Festival (see page 40 for suggestions)

Day IV-VI

- Do the "Me" mini-unit, pages 57-63.

Day VII

- Plan and prepare for an Open House to culminate the Self-Esteem Unit

Overview of Activities
SETTING THE STAGE

1. Make a display of Care of Teeth materials; e.g., toothbrush, toothpaste, dental floss, electric toothbrush, mouthwash, fluoride rinse, irrigator machine, dental tools (if a loan from a dentist can be arranged).

2. Invite a dental care worker or the school nurse to speak to the class. Be sure the talk includes the importance of good nutrition to dental care.

3. Language experience story–"Dental Care." Have students tell what they learned from the visitor while you record their comments. The narrative may be illustrated and sent to the visitor as a thank you after the children have had a chance to enjoy it for a few days.

4. Have students draw or write four things they can do to care for their teeth (e.g., brush, visit the dentist, drink milk, eat healthy foods).

5. Use "Good or Bad for Teeth" activity sheet (page 37) and Dental Care Dot-to-Dot (page 38).

6. Make a Living Graph, "How Many Teeth Have You Lost?" See page 52 for general instructions.

7. Learn and sing "Brush Your Teeth." (See Bibliography, page 80, for source.)

Overview of Activities *(cont.)*

ENJOYING THE STORY

1. Read "The Tooth" for enjoyment.

2. Discuss self-esteem concepts–feeling self-conscious, respecting and taking good care of your body.

   Focus on feelings–being upset, hurt, embarrassed, and sympathetic.
   1. *What happened to George when he was roller skating?*
   2. *What can you do to protect yourself when you are playing?*
   3. *How did the dentist help George?*
   4. *How was Martha a good friend?*
   5. *Should you always tell the truth even when it might hurt someone's feelings?*

3. Make a TV movie.

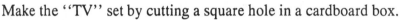

   Make the "TV" set by cutting a square hole in a cardboard box.
   Cut slits on either side of the box.
   Cut drawing paper to size of hole.
   Discuss what happened in the story.
   Print the events in order on a chart.
   Organize groups and help each group choose an event.
   Each group draws and colors one event on a piece of drawing paper.
   A group could be chosen to make the title page.
   Put the drawings in the right order.
   Paste them together to make a long strip.
   Tape the edges of the strip to reinforce.
   Watch the movie!
   A narrator could be chosen to retell the story as it unrolls.

4. Make puppet plays of the story.

EXTENDING THE STORY

1. Have students draw, write, or tell about a time when they were hurt. Let them share their stories.

2. Do "Fill the Hat" activity sheet, page 39.

3. Study real hippopotamuses. Make sure students compare pictures of George and Martha with pictures of real hippos.

4. Do math activity, "Hippo Puzzle," pages 50 and 51.

5. Culminate your George and Martha unit with a Friendship Festival Day. See page 40 for suggested activities.

Good or Bad for Teeth

Put an X on the things that are bad for your teeth.

Color the things that are good for your teeth.

Name_____

Dental Care Dot-to-Dot

1.   Join the dots to make a picture.

2.   Color it.

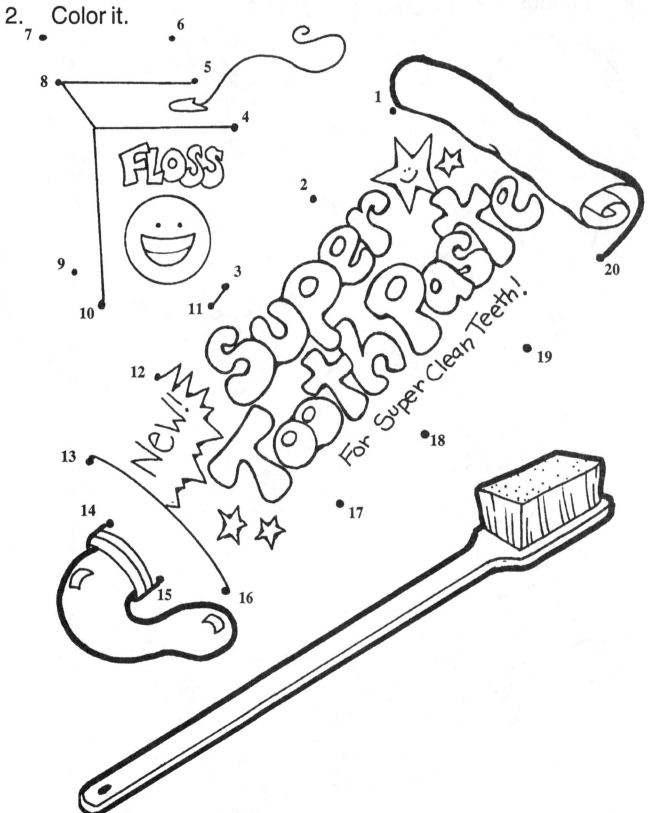

Fill the Hat

1. Cut out the pictures that start with **Hh.**

2. Paste them on George's hat.

Friendship Festival

Get Ready

People are by nature social animals. The ability to make friends is highly correlated to self-esteem. Friends affirm feelings of self-worth and acceptance. Therefore, helping children to understand friendship is well worth the effort.

Group Discussions
''What Is A Friend?''
''Why Do We Need Friends?''
''How To Make Friends''
''I Like Friends''

Play ''Hand Squeeze''
Sit in a circle.
Hold hands.
Send a hand squeeze around the circle.

Have a Group Hug
Ask 4 or 5 children to stand up.
Ask them to hug each other all
in a bunch at the same time.

Make a Big Book

• Read Joan Walsh Anglund's, *A Friend Is Someone Who Likes You* to the children. Give each child a piece of paper with the language pattern from the book on it (or have them copy it):

A friend is someone who _____.

Have children dictate or write the words to complete the sentence and illustrate it. Display the pages around the room for all to enjoy for a few days; then bind into a Big Book for the class library.

• One way to make a sturdy Big Book is to lay the pages next to each other. Tape the touching edges together using wide, non-yellowing, clear tape. You now have a long strip of pages. Add a title page to the left end. Fold, accordion fashion into book form–title page on the front and other pages back to back. Staple close to the back edge being sure to catch all the pages. Cover the staples with tape.

Make Booklets

Using page 43 as the cover and as many copies of page 44 as needed for inside pages, have children make booklets called ''My Friends.'' Inside pages could include a list of friends' names, why a special friend is liked, ways friends help each other, etc. Be sure these are shared with classmates and at the Open House.

Hot Tip!
Watch for children who feel they don't have any friends.
Plan how to help them.

Poems for *George and Martha*

An excellent collection of children's poetry on almost any subject is ***Read-Aloud Rhymes for the Very Young,*** selected by Jack Prelutsky (Knopf, 1986). The poems mentioned below are from this book unless otherwise noted.

"Split Pea Soup"

- Use "The Meal" to introduce a discussion of foods that are liked and disliked, pointing out that what one person likes, another may dislike. "Crunch and Lick" is about foods that most people like and "Table Manners" could be used to set the mood for a well-mannered tasting party.

- The poem "Turtle Soup" by Lewis Carroll (reprinted in *The Random House Book of Poetry for Children,* see Bibliography, page 80) describes a beautiful green soup; without the title you'd never know it wasn't pea soup!

"The Flying Machine"

- The poems "Big" and "The Wish" are about growing.

- You may wish to display "Something About Me" (below) at your measuring station.

Something About Me

There's something about me
That I'm knowing.
There's something about me
That isn't showing.
I'm growing!

The Balloon

1st Group: What's the news of the day,
Good neighbor, I pray?

2nd Group: They say the balloon
Has gone up to the moon.

- "Wouldn't You?" and "A Kite" are two poems about flying. The Mother Goose rhyme "The Balloon" (above) would be fun to learn as a two-part chant.

"The Tub"

- When discussing bathtime, any or all of the following poems could be used: "Before the Bath," "Naughty Soap Song," "The Way They Scrub," "Wish," and "Happy Winter, Steamy Tub."

- "Blowing Bubbles" is an excellent rhyme to learn and chant while doing the "Let's Play With Bubbles!" activities, page 56.

"The Mirror"

- A poem about looking in a mirror is "Robert, Who Is Often a Stranger to Himself."

"The Tooth"

- A poem to use when discussing good dental practices, is "Toothsome" about the use of toothpaste.

- The Mother Goose riddle rhyme "The Teeth" can be introduced to the children without the title. Have them guess what the poem is describing. Supply the title after discussion and let them demonstrate the poem!

The Teeth
Thirty white horses
Upon a red hill;
Now they stamp,
Now they champ,
Now they stand still.

Helping Young Children Begin to Write

Language Experience Stories

Following selected unit activities, have children talk about their experiences. Record their responses on chart paper and label with the provider's name for a great esteem builder. Over the course of a short period of time, make sure all children are represented. (Use the Class Record Form, page 78, to check off names.) These "stories" can be illustrated and displayed around the classroom.

Here are some specific suggestions for topics from the *George and Martha* activities:

Foods I Hate and Love, page 7	Bathtime Safety, page 22
Tasting Party, page 7	Mirror Play, pages 28 and 29
Cooking and Baking, page 7	Funny Reflections, page 29
I am Growing!, page 12	Dental Worker Visit, page 35
Seen from the Air, page 13	Caring for My Teeth, page 35
Flying activities, page 13	When I Was Hurt, page 36
Water and Bubble Play, pages 22 and 23	A Friend is Someone Who..., page 40

Helping Children Write Their Own Stories

Level One:

The child illustrates story while waiting for help.
The child dictates to teacher, a parent helper, or an older child.
The "secretary" then reads the story back to the child.
The child then practices telling the story.

Level Two:

The child illustrates story while waiting for help.
The child dictates to a "secretary" who prints the story on the blackboard.
The child then copies it.

Level Three:

The child prints own story to the best of his/her ability.
Encourage the use of pictionary books, charts, Big Books for spelling help.
Child illustrates story.
The child reads the story to teacher.
Suggest corrections for only one or two words.

Level Four:

The child needs little help and is inspired.
Focus on the quality of ideas, not spelling or printing.
Ask the child to read story to listeners.
Suggest a few corrections.
Provide adequate materials and time.

42

Martha

Color.

Cut out.

May be used as a book cover.

43

Martha *(cont.)*

Cut out.

Use for book pages.

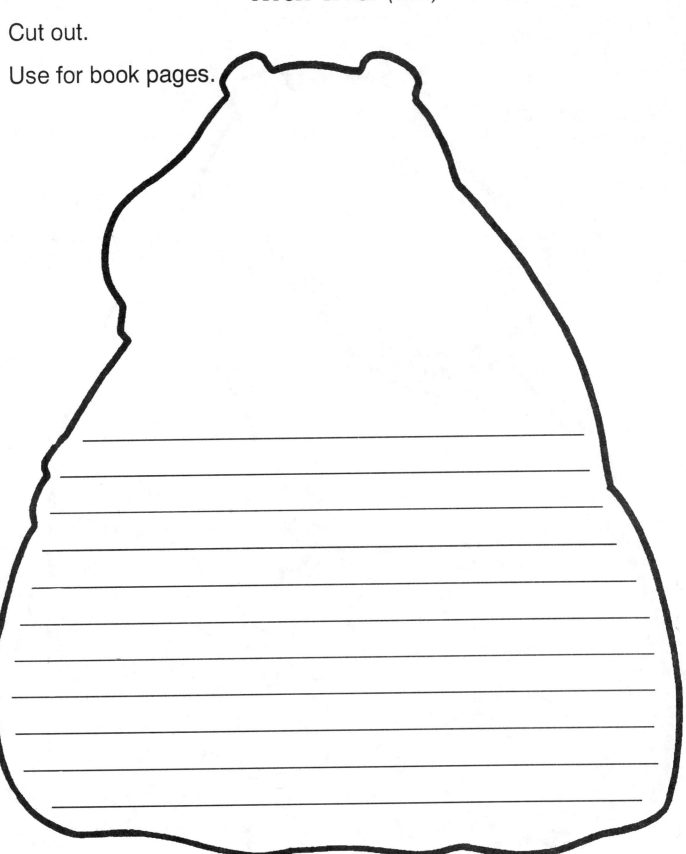

44

Creative Drama

The *George and Martha* stories are ideal for creative drama activities. Each story is simple and short, with lots of action and dialogue. Have fun!

Using Puppets

Materials:

George and Martha puppets (Directions and patterns for paper bag puppets are on pages 64 and 65. Directions and patterns for stick puppets are on pages 46–48).

Puppet Stage

Teacher Preparation:

1. **Rules For Creative Drama**—Have a class discussion to decide the rules. Include a discussion about being too rough with the puppets and polite audience behavior. Print the rules on a chart and display it in the Creative Drama Center.

2. **Make a Puppet Stage**

   Table – Hang an old sheet over a table.
   The puppeteers simply kneel on the floor behind the table.
   The puppets move on top of the table.

   Box – Cut a large square hole in the top half of a big box.
   Prop up the box securely.
   The puppeteers sit or kneel behind the box.
   The puppets move in the square hole.
   Simple curtains could be made by hanging a string across at the top of the square hole.

   Sheet – Hang a heavy rope across a corner of the room.
   Drape a sheet over the string.
   The puppeteers kneel behind the sheet, in the corner.
   The puppets move above the sheet.

Directions For The Children:

1. Choose a partner.

2. Think about George and Martha. How do they move? How do they talk?

3. Think about what happened in the story.

   Use the Story Retelling Activity to help you remember.

4. Plan your play.

5. Practice it.

6. Make a big sign to tell the title of your play.

7. Share your puppet play with other children.

Story Retelling Activities

Choose one of the activities below to use for retelling the George and Martha stories.

Clothesline

Materials: Clothesline or thick string; clothespins; story props (pages 47–49)

Teacher Preparation:

Copy the story props onto heavy paper.
Color with marking pens.
Cut out and laminate.
Hang the clothesline (between two chairs, across a corner, etc.).
Provide containers for clothespins and story props.

Directions For The Child:

Retell the story while hanging the story props in sequence.

Flannel or Magnetic Board

Materials: Flannel board; felt or sandpaper; story props (pages 47–49)

Teacher Preparation:

Use carbon paper to trace patterns onto felt.
Decorate with permanent ink marking pens.
Cut out.
OR
Copy the patterns onto heavy paper.
Color with marking pens.
Cut out.

Glue pieces of felt or sandpaper to back of each for use on flannel board or attach self-stick magnetic strips (available in craft stores) for use on magnetic board.

Provide a container for story props.

Directions For The Child:

Retell the story using the story props on the flannel or magnetic board.

Stick Puppets

Materials: Tongue depressors and/or craft sticks; story props (pages 47–49); puppet stage (see page 45 for suggestions)

Teacher Preparation:

Copy the story props onto heavy paper.
Color with marking pens.
Cut out and laminate.
Attach (staple or tape) a tongue depressor or craft stick.
Provide a container for story props.

Directions For The Child:

Retell the story with a puppet show.

46

Story Retelling Props

*See page 46 for suggested activities.

Story Retelling Props *(cont.)*

*See page 46 for suggested activities.

*You may wish to make more than one George so he can be shown minus a tooth and with a gold tooth.

48

Story Retelling Props *(cont.)*

*See page 46 for suggested activities.

Cut out this space for Martha's window.

Decorate one side as her bathroom and the other side as the outside of her house.

Additional Props

1. Use the project on pages 18 and 19 for George in his flying machine.

2. Prepare a second flying machine with an empty basket.

3. Use the tub on page 27.

4. Make a full-length mirror by gluing a 7'' x 4'' (17.5 x 10 cm) piece of foil onto an 8'' x 5'' (20 x 12.5cm) piece of construction paper.

Hippo Puzzle

Name _____

Can you read the numbers?

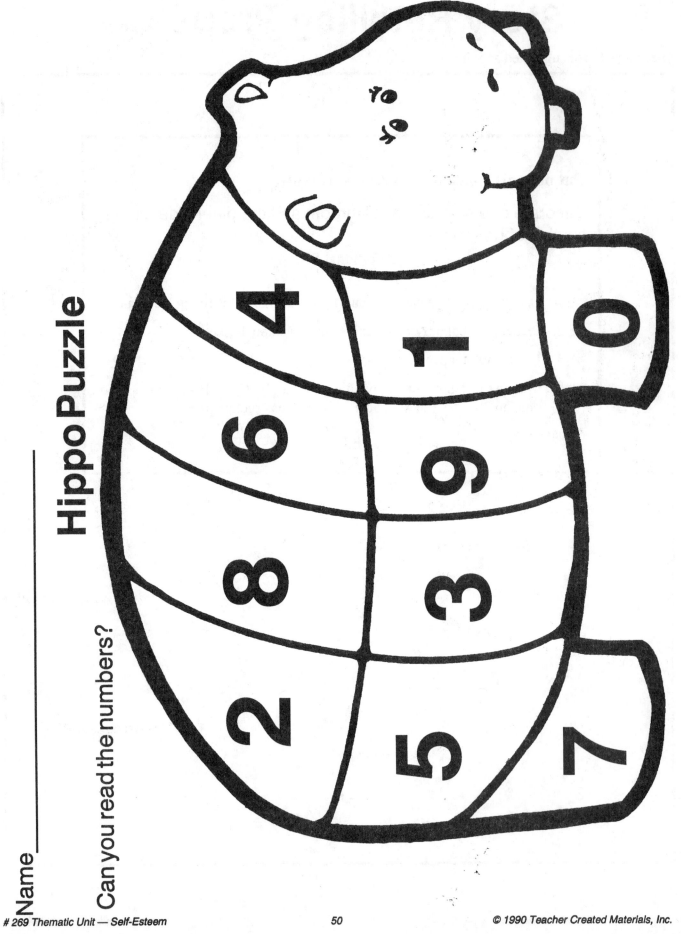

50

HippoPuzzle (cont.)

Name

1. Cut out.
2. Match to Hippo.
3. Paste onto Hippo.

Living Graphs

Below are general directions for making these adaptable teaching tools. They should be assembled and interpreted as a group activity with all children participating.

Teacher Preparation

1. Make the graph form on chart paper (see samples below).

2. Cut the small pieces of paper to be added to the graph. Use a separate color for each variable on the graph. The size of these pieces depends on the activity. They should be large enough for children to write their name or initials. Small self-stick notes may be used.

Making the Graph

1. Work with small groups at a time.

2. Help children choose the correct color graphing piece, add their names or initials, and glue to graph (a glue stick minimizes mess) under the appropriate heading. Be sure to include your own name!

Interpreting the Graph

1. When everyone has added their piece to the graph, call the group together to study it.

2. Have the children represented in one section stand up. Count them. Count the number of paper pieces in that section. Help children see that each piece of paper stands for one person.

3. Have children tell which section has the most, the fewest.

4. Depending on the abilities of the children, make problems to solve from the graph. For example, how many children have green eyes or how many more children have blue eyes than brown eyes?

Sample Graphs

What Color Are My Eyes?

Brown	☐☐☐☐☐☐☐☐☐
Blue	☐☐☐☐☐
Green	☐☐☐

How Many Letters In Your Name?

M	A	R	G	A	R	E	T
H	E	L	G	A			
J	U	L	I	A	N		
J	O	E					
H	O						
E	R	N	E	S	T	I	N	E
F	R	A	N	K	L	I	N
M	A	R	Y				
E	D						
D	E	B	B	I	E		
T	H	U	Y				

What month is your birthday In?

										Dara	
						David			Grant		
Staci	Terry		Tina		Ed			Keith	Chris	Nik	Pal
Jan.	Feb.	Mar.	Apr.	May	June	July	Aug.	Sep.	Oct.	Nov.	Dec.

Additional Graphing Topics

- Hair color
- How many teeth have you lost?
- What letter does your name begin with?

- How old are you?
- How many in your family?
- My favorite dessert

Make a Parachute

You will need:

thread   plastic bag cut open   clothespin

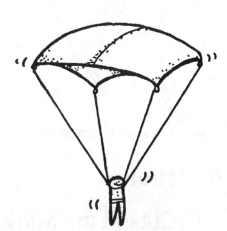

Directions:

1. Cut 4 pieces of thread 1 foot long.

2. Tie the thread to the corners of the plastic bag.

3. Tie the ends of the threads together.
    Then tie them to the clothespin.

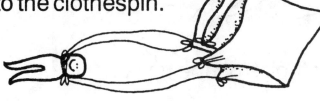

4. Lay it all out very straight.
    Roll it up carefully.
    Hold it in your hand.

CAN YOU MAKE IT FLY?

Make a Twirly

You will need:

 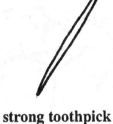 

cork   **strong toothpick**   scissors   tape

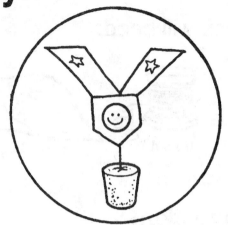

Directions:

1. Cut out the twirly bird shape.

2. Cut on the .... line.

3. Fold like this.

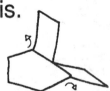

4. Tape the toothpick on the x x x x.

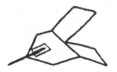

5. Push the toothpick into the cork.

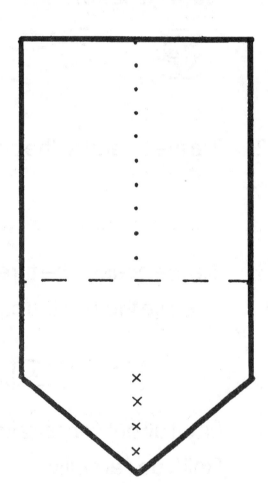

CAN YOU MAKE IT FLY?

Make George Go Up

You will need:

balloon

Directions:

1. Color George.

   Cut him out.

   Cut out the **+**.

   Pull the balloon through the **+**.

George

2. Have an adult blow up the balloon as big as possible.

3. Hold the balloon this way.

   Let go!

   What happens?

4. Hold the balloon this way.

   Let go!

   What happens?

 # 269 Thematic Unit — Self-Esteem

Let's Play With Bubbles!

Bath of Bubbles

Materials:
Plastic tub or dishpan
Plastic sheet or tablecloth
Newspapers
Water
Dishwashing soap
Straws
Pail

Teacher Preparation:

Spread the plastic sheet on the tabletop.
Spread the newspapers on the floor (so it won't get slippery).
Make the bubble solution:

Measure 10 cups water into a pail.
Add 1 cup of dishwashing soap.
Add 3 tablespoons glycerine (optional).
Stir gently, a little bit.
If you get ''froth'' on the top, skim it off.
Fill the tub 1/4 inch deep with the solution.

Directions For The Children:

Dip your straw into the solution. Pull it out gently.
Hold the tip of the straw just above the surface of the solution.
Blow softly.

Listen to bubbles. Smell bubbles.

Look at the shapes and colors of bubbles.
Can you build bubbles into a pile?
Touch bubbles. What happens?
Can you touch a bubble without popping it?

Outside Bubble Fun

Materials:
Several large plastic tubs or small wading pool containing bubble solution
Plastic six-pack holders
Coat hangers pulled into a circle shape
Bubble wands

HAVE FUN MAKING BIG BUBBLES!

56

"Me" Mini-Unit

This mini-unit could be used to introduce the topic of self-esteem or as a concluding project following the *George and Martha* activities. At least three days will be needed to complete all the activities.

Bulletin Board

Prepare and use the "Child of the Day" bulletin board. Complete directions and patterns are on pages 73 to 75.

Discussion Topics

Show And Tell:
Encourage the children to bring something from home that they have made, or collected, or learned about.
Teach the other children to be good listeners and to treat the treasure with respect.
Set up a Center to display these treasures.
Ensure that all the children eventually have a turn.

Sharing Time:
Provide many opportunities for the children to talk about themselves, their interests, their families and their feelings.
Help them to reflect, compare, and draw conclusions about their own experiences and those of others.
An interesting topic might be, "Tell about your name."

Group Discussions:
Ask the children to discuss a given topic. Encourage all the children to participate, and accept all ideas. Record some of their ideas on a big chart. Then read the chart aloud while the children watch for their contribution. Display the chart and review it the next day. After you have 3 or 4 charts, make them into a Big Book. Encourage the children to illustrate their Big Book.

Art Projects

See pages 62 and 63 for suggestions and directions.

Songs

Learn and sing "I'm Just Me" and/or "I Believe in Me." (See Bibliography, page 80, for source.)

Poems

See page 67 for Body Awareness poems and activities. Use "Jump or Jiggle" from *Read-Aloud Poems for the Very Young* (see Bibliography, page 80). Create movements to go with words. Change the last word to other movements children can do.

"Me" Mini-Unit (cont.)

Physical Challenge Activities

See page 66 for suggestions and directions.

Language Activities

Picture Puzzle

Ask the parents to send a large photo of their child.

Photocopy it and then return it to the parent.

Mount the photocopy on heavy paper and laminate.

Then cut it up into a simple jigsaw puzzle.

Put the child's initials on the back of each piece.

Put the pieces in an envelope labelled "Guess Who?"

Let the children have fun doing the puzzles and guessing who it is.

Who Is It?

Ask the children to bring a photograph of themselves as a baby to school in a "secret envelope," showing no one.

Display the photographs on a bulletin board labelled "Who Is It?"

Include a photograph of yourself as a baby!

Give the children opportunities to guess who.

After a few days, ask the children to make a label with their name on it and staple these under the correct photographs.

Who Am I?

Ask one child to sit on a chair with her back to the class and hide her eyes.

Another child is silently picked to come up and stand behind her, and say "Who Am I?" in a normal voice.

The first child has three tries to guess who it is.

Then another child has a turn.

"I Like You Because...."

Ask the children to sit in a circle.

Take turns saying, "I like you because..." to the person on the left, on the right, or across. The teacher can play too.

Make A Class Book

Make a class book called "Who Am I?"

Use older children or buddies as scribes.

The children illustrate and dictate their own page.

Assemble the pages. You may wish to use wallpaper samples for the cover.

Make A "Me" Booklet

Reproduce pages 59–61 for each child.

Cut each page in half and assemble into a booklet by stapling the left edges. Add blank pages if you wish.

Use parent volunteers or older children, if you wish, to aid you in helping each child complete his booklet.

Drawings may be used in place of, or in addition to, writing.

ME

by _____

I am special!

I am _____ years
old. Next I will be
_____ years old.

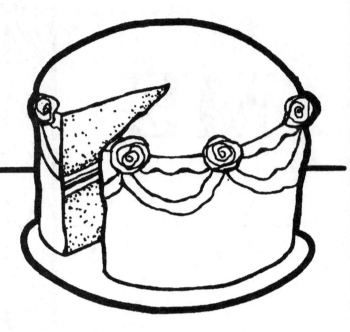

Draw candles on the cake to show how old you are.

- **cut here** - - - - - -

I am a good helper.

**I am smart.
I can color the
rainbow.**

red

yellow

blue

Write your name BIG on one cloud and
little on the other.

- - - - - - - - - - - - - - cut here -

I know...

61

"Me" Art Activities

Happy Hands

Materials:

Drawing paper
Crayons or felt tip pens

Directions:

The child traces his hand onto paper.
He then decorates the hand tracing to make a happy or silly face.
Several happy hands can be made on one paper.

Foot Faces

Materials:

As above.

Directions:

As above, only the child traces his foot onto paper.
The foot faces can be cut out and displayed
as "tracks" around the classroom.

Body Prints

Materials:

tempera paint in deep aluminum pie plates
newspaper
pail of soapy water and a towel
paper

Directions:

Organize the children into small groups.
Spread out newspaper for each group.
Put a set of materials for each group on the newspaper.
The children make a fingerprint by dipping their finger in
    the paint, blotting it on the newspaper, and then
    printing on the paper. They then wash their finger.
Then they can make a handprint and a footprint.
Let the prints dry, then discuss the uniqueness of each
    person's print.
Display the prints.

"Me" Art Activities *(cont.)*

Body Pictures

Materials:

large sheets of paper; felt tip pens; crayons; pencils; scraps of yarn, construction paper, fabric, etc.

Directions For The Child:

Lie down on a large piece of paper.

Be as still as you can.

Ask a friend to trace around you with a pencil or crayon.

Decorate your body picture to look just like you.

Ways To Use Body Pictures:

1. Cut out the body pictures and display down the hall, or around the room.

2. Make a sculpture. Cut out the body picture, then trace around it to make a second outline. Cut it out, too.

   Staple the outlines together and stuff with newspaper.

   Sit the body sculpture in a desk, on the windowsill, etc.

3. Do not cut out the body picture.

   Instead, help the child measure the parts of his body.

   Write the measurements on the body picture.

   This could be done in small groups.

4. Ask the children to trace around your body. Decorate and cut out.

   Cut your body picture into parts to make a puzzle.

5. Print the names of the body parts on the teacher body picture.

Crowns

Materials:

paper grocery bags (each bag will make 2 crowns); scissors; stapler; felt pens; aluminum foil cut-outs from pie plates; ribbon; wool; shape stickers; scraps of wrapping paper; fabric scraps

Teacher Preparation:

Flatten the bag. Cut off the bottom. Fold in half.

Draw the pattern for the crown as shown in the diagram.

Cut it out.

Adjust the size of the crown to fit the child's head and staple.

Print the child's name on the back of the crown.

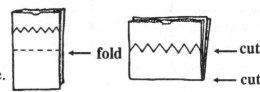

Directions For The Child:

Color the crown.

Decorate it.

Wear the crown to show how special you are!

Or use it for dress-up. Are you a King or Queen?

A Prince or Princess?

Make a Puppet

Materials:

paper lunch bags
paste
scissors
crayons or felt pens

Directions:

1. Color the patterns.
2. Cut out.
3. Paste in place on the paper bag.
4. Color a mouth under the flap.
5. Choose to make either one or both of the puppets.

Patterns For George

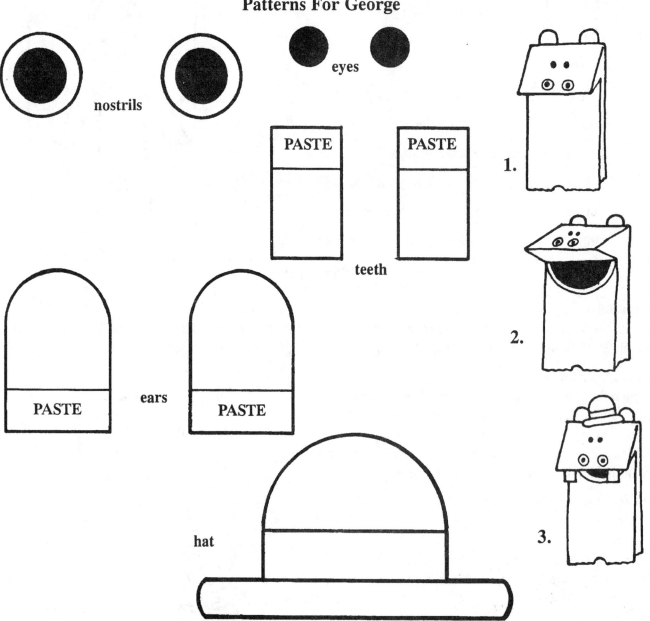

nostrils

eyes

teeth

ears

hat

1.

2.

3.

Make a Puppet *(cont.)*

Patterns For Martha

nostrils

eyes

 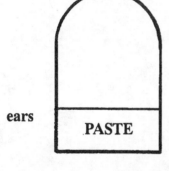

ears

PASTE

PASTE

teeth

skirt

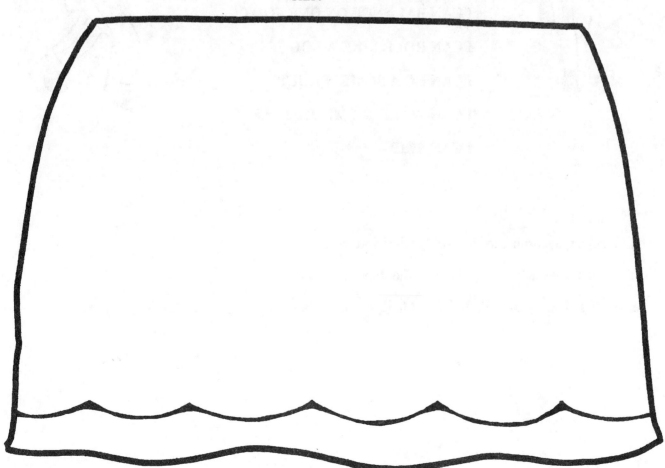

Physical Challenge Activities

Ask the children to practice the following skills.

Be sure to encourage and praise whenever possible.

Watch for those children who are working hard to improve their skills.

Hand out awards to those who show improvement or acquire a new skill.

Use the award forms in the Unit Management Section (page 77).

I CAN THROW A BALL

I CAN CATCH A BALL

I CAN SKIP

I CAN HOP ON ONE FOOT

I CAN TOUCH MY TOES

I CAN BALANCE ON ONE FOOT

I CAN ROLL LIKE A LOG

I CAN DO A SOMERSAULT

I CAN WALK ON MY TIPTOES

I CAN SKIP

Add to the list, according to the skill level of your class.

Do these activities now and again throughout the entire unit.

Use the Class Record Form in the Unit Management section (page 78) to keep track of progress.

66

Body Awareness Action Poems

I'm a Special Person

(To the tune of ''I'm a Little Teapot'')

I'm a special person, there's just one me,
I can run so fast I seem to fly....   (let the children run around the gym)
I'm a special person, there's just one me,
Jump so high I can touch the sky....   (let the children jump about the gym)

Chin, Elbows, Toes

(To the tune of ''Three Blind Mice'')

Chin, elbows, toes,   (children touch the body parts)

Chin, elbows, toes,

Shins, tummy, nose,

Shins, tummy, nose,

Sit down, stand up and turn around twice.... (give them time to do it)

Sit down, stand up and turn around twice....

Sit down, stand up and turn around twice....

Chin, elbows, toes.

Body Touch

Touch your fingers,   Touch your hips,
Touch your nose,   Touch your elbows,
Touch your ears,   Touch your knees,
And now your toes!   And now your toes!

(Ask the children to think of other body parts to touch, and make up more verses.)

Poems by Diane Williams

Let's Cook

These general directions will help you get ready for any cooking project and, in particular, the preparation of split pea soup and chocolate chip cookies. Cooking with children is an ambitious activity during which you and your helper must be at the controls. The children are involved in measuring, mixing, smelling and eating.

Teacher Preparation:

1. Arrange for a helper to come (a parent or other adult volunteer).
2. Print the rules on a chart.
3. Print the recipe on a chart (see page 69).
4. Read the Rules Chart to the class and discuss.
5. Organize at least 2 small groups. Prepare a separate batch for each group.
6. Spread out newspaper or plastic tablecloth.
7. Put out all the equipment and ingredients.

Baking and Cooking Rules
1. Wash your hands.
2. Wear an apron or cover-up.
3. Ask a grown-up to help.
4. Take turns.
5. Measure carefully.
6. Help clean up.

Directions:

1. Put the recipe chart where it is easily seen.
2. Ensure the other children are busy and supervised.
3. Take the cooking group to a table. Play ''Guess what it is!'' by closing eyes and smelling each ingredient.
4. Read the recipe to your group a bit at a time.
5. Give each child a turn to add an ingredient or stir.
6. Cook or bake.
7. Have a Tasting Party!

For Soup:

Serve with crackers or croutons in reusable plastic cups.
Give each child just a taste.
Discuss why you should try something before deciding if you like it or not.
Ask 2 children to take a cup of soup to the principal.
Ask them to watch if the principal tries it!
Save the rest of the soup to freeze for Open House.

For Cookies:

Ask 2 children to take a plate of cookies to the principal.
Count the chocolate chips in the cookies and graph (see page 7).
Save enough cookies to freeze for Open House.

Martha's Favorite Recipes

Split Pea Soup

Ingredients:

2 cups dried split peas (500 mL)
8 cups water (2 L)
1 medium onion, chopped
1 teaspoon salt (5 mL)
2 medium carrots, chopped
2 medium celery stalks, chopped

Equipment:

Stove or hot plate or slow cooking pot
Measuring cups and spoons
Dutch oven or soup pot with lid
Wooden spoon
Oven mitts
Soup ladle
Knife and cutting board
Reusable plastic cups and spoons

Directions:

Measure peas and water into pot. Heat to boiling; boil 2 minutes.

Remove from heat; cover and let stand for 1 hour. (Teacher may wish to do these steps ahead of time.)

Stir onion and salt into peas. Heat to boiling; reduce heat.

Cover and simmer until peas are tender, about 1 hour.

Stir carrots and celery into soup. Heat to boiling; reduce heat.

Cover and simmer until vegetables are tender, about 45 minutes. Makes 8 regular servings.

Options:

1. Make the soup in a slow cooker. Add all the ingredients at once. Cook 6-8 hours or until peas are tender. May be reheated and served the next day.
2. Heat and taste canned pea soup.

Chocolate Chip Cookies

Ingredients:

1/2 cup sugar (125 mL)
1/2 cup packed brown sugar (125 mL)
1/3 cup margarine or butter, softened (75 mL)
1/3 cup shortening (75 mL)
1 egg
1 teaspoon vanilla (5 mL)
1 1/2 cups flour (or whole wheat flour) (375 mL)
1/2 teaspoon baking soda (2.5 mL)
1/2 teaspoon salt (2.5 mL)
1 package (6 oz.) chocolate chips (170 g)

Equipment:

Oven
Measuring cups and spoons
Large and small mixing bowl
Wooden spoon
Cookie sheets or oblong pan
Teaspoons
Oven mitts
Spatula
Cooling racks
Plates

Directions:

Heat oven to 375° F (190° C). Mix sugars, margarine, shortening, egg, and vanilla until smooth and creamy. Stir in remaining ingredients.

Drop dough by rounded teaspoonfuls about 2 inches apart onto ungreased cookie sheet. Bake until light brown, 8 to 10 minutes. Cool slightly before removing from cookie sheet with spatula. Cool on racks. Makes about 40 cookies.

Options:

1. Bake as bar cookies. Spread dough in greased oblong (13 x 9 1/2 x 2'') pan. Bake at 375° F (190° C) for 20 to 25 minutes.
2. Bake purchased prepared cookie dough.
3. Taste purchased chocolate chip cookies.

An Open House

When using a whole language, thematic approach it is important to get the full support of the parents. They need to see that learning this way is challenging, productive, fun, and successful. One way to share the children's accomplishments is to have an Open House.

Plan to have the Open House after you have completed the Self-Esteem Unit. The easiest time is during the school day. This limits the number of guests to those who are not at work, and puts you in total control since it is during school time. The more ambitious time is in the evening. This increases the chance that all children will be able to "perform" for their families.

Plan

1. **Explain to the children what an open house is.**

   Tell them it is a fun way to share school with their families.

   Explain it is a chance to show all they have learned.

2. **Ask the children which activities they'd like to share.**

   Explain that everyone will share at least one activity.

   Using the Activity List, page 72, ask what they would like to share.

3. **Audition for each activity.**

   Praise, encourage, and enjoy this class sharing.

   Discreetly jot down your evaluations, using the Activity List.

   Do all your selections in private later.

   Omit some activities if necessary.

   Make sure that everyone is sharing at least one activity.

   (Use page 72 to note assignments.)

Open House Assignments		
Puppets	Props	Art
James	Tami	Jocelyn
Dara	Don	Chau
Matt	Felipe	Autumn

4. **Tell each child what he/she will share.**

   Be flexible. Remember the Open House is for fun.

   If there is a problem, work at a compromise.

An Open House *(cont.)*

Prepare

1. Give the children time to prepare and practice.

2. Prepare some group presentations such as songs, poems.

3. Print the program on a chart, include performers' names.

4. Send out the invitations.

5. Tidy the activity centers. Add new materials if necessary.

   Encourage the children to teach their families how to do the activities.

6. Display children's work attractively.

7. Plan the seating. Ask the children how many guests they are bringing.

8. Have a dress rehearsal. Share the presentation with another class.

9. Practice showing imaginary families around the room. Ask the children to find the things they would like to show their families. Ask them to plan how they will teach their families at the Activity Centers.

Please Come
To Our Open House
We have just finished studying
Very Important People–Ourselves!
We would like to share with you.
Place:
Date:
Time:

Have Fun!

Remember it is the process, not the product that counts now. Families have few opportunities to see their children perform, so they will appreciate your efforts, and they will enjoy the Open House!

Remember to use the Open House as an opportunity to reinforce self-esteem – both yours and the children's.

Then, when it is all done, confess that you were nervous too.

And join the children in a celebration:

We are Brave!
We are Smart!
We are Special!

We Did It!

Open House Presentations

George and Martha

"Split Pea Soup"

_____ 1. Retell story with props

_____ 2. Puppet Play–with paper bag puppets

_____ 3. Creative Drama–with costumes

_____ 4. Let's Bake Cookies–explain, share recipe

_____ 5. Let's Cook Soup–explain, share recipe

_____ 6. "Eat It Up", "Brussel Sprouts," or "Biscuits in the Oven"–class sings song together

"The Flying Machine"

_____ 1. Measuring–explain, share an activity

_____ 2. Retell story with props

_____ 3. Puppet Play

_____ 4. Creative Drama

_____ 5. "Up, Up, Up"–share story

_____ 6. "I Must Be Growing," "I Wonder If I'm Growing," or "I Can Fly"–class sings song together

"The Tub"

_____ 1. Retell story with props

_____ 2. Puppet Play

_____ 3. Creative Drama

_____ 4. Play With Bubbles–explain activities

_____ 5. "Crowded Tub"–class sings song together

"The Mirror"

_____ 1. Retell story with props

_____ 2. Puppet Plays

_____ 3. Creative Drama

_____ 4. Play With Mirrors–explain activities

_____ 5. Show sequence stories

"The Tooth"

_____ 1. "The Dentist"–share story

_____ 2. Retell story with the movie

_____ 3. Puppet Play

_____ 4. Creative Drama

_____ 5. "Ouch"–share story

_____ 6. "Brush Your Teeth"–class sings song together

My Friends

_____ 1. Share a chart about friends

_____ 2. Big Book "What Is a Friend?"– read aloud

_____ 3. "My Friends" booklet–share

_____ 4. "A Good Friend" or "Friends"–class sings song together

Me

_____ 1. "Me" booklet–share a favorite page

_____ 2. Big Book about "Me"–read aloud

_____ 3. Big Book about "Who Am I?"–read aloud

_____ 4. "I'm Just Me" or "I Believe in Me"–class sings song together

72

"Child of the Day" Bulletin Board

Objective

This bulletin board enhances a child's self-esteem by making him/her the center of attention for a day.

Materials

- Light-colored background paper
- One sheet 18 x 24'' construction paper, wrapping paper, wallpaper, etc. for frame (pattern, page 74)
- Brightly colored construction paper for balloons (pattern, page 75)
- Colored string or yarn for balloon strings
- Picture of child (see below for suggestions)
- Staples or pushpins
- Index cards or construction paper strips

Construction

- Reproduce or trace patterns onto construction paper. (Shiny foil wrapping paper or patterned wallpaper make striking frames.) Cut out.
- Label balloons as you wish (see sample for suggestions).
- Assemble the pieces and attach to bulletin board with pushpins or staples. Add strings to balloons.
- Store index cards nearby. Fill in and attach to bulletin board each day.

Directions

- Choose a child of the day (alphabetical order, draw names, etc.).
- Put the child's picture in the frame. The picture may be one brought from home or an extra copy of a school picture. Or, try one of these esteem-building options: 1. Use a camera with self-developing film to produce an on-the-spot photo. 2. Have the child stand sideways between a strong light source (a filmstrip or overhead projector work well but caution the child not to look into the light) and a piece of black construction paper taped to the wall. Trace around the shadow of his/her head, cut out, and frame this silhouette on the bulletin board.
- Interview the child in front of the whole class and fill in an index card with the child's answers. (Help with phone number and address if necessary. This activity is a good incentive for learning this vital information.) Attach to appropriate balloon.
- Make the child's day extra special. Let him/her be line leader, message carrier, sit next to the teacher, etc. If the children are capable, have them write stories about or letters to the child of the day using the information on the cards.

Bulletin Board Patterns

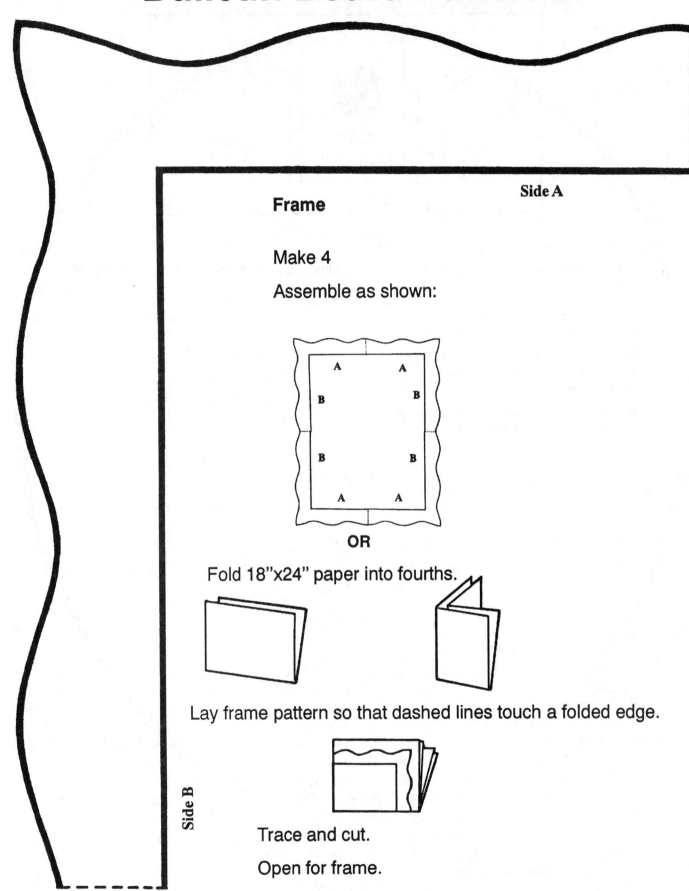

Side A

Frame

Make 4

Assemble as shown:

OR

Fold 18"x24" paper into fourths.

Lay frame pattern so that dashed lines touch a folded edge.

Side B

Trace and cut.

Open for frame.

74

Bulletin Board Patterns *(cont.)*

Balloon

Reproduce 6, each
in a different bright
color.

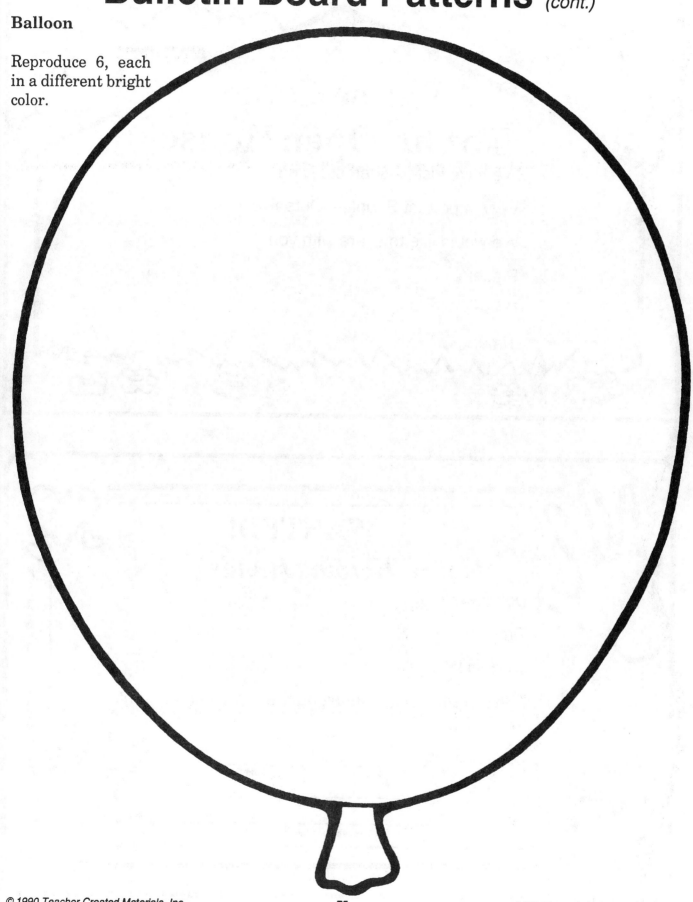

Please Come To Our Open House!

We have just finished studying

Very Important People—Ourselves!

We would like to share with you.

Place:

Date:

Time:

WANTED!
Helping Hands

Date:

Time:

To Help With:

Please return with your signature if you can help with this activity.

I can help on _____ at _____
             date   time

_____
         signature

_____
       phone number

SPECIAL PERSON AWARD!

To:

For:

From:

I Did Something Great!

Class Record Form

Name																								

Request for Ingredients

Dear Parents,

Please help with our

cooking project by sending

_____
ingredients

on or before _____
date

Thank you,

Hungry Hippo

and _____

Bibliography

Books

Aliki. *We Are Best Friends.* Greenwillow, 1982

Anglund, Joan Walsh. *A Friend Is Someone Who Likes You.* HBJ, 1983

Aruego, Jose. *Look What I Can Do.* Macmillan, 1988

Burningham, John. *The Friend.* Thomas & Crowell, 1976

Carle, Eric. *Do You Want To Be My Friend?* Crowell Jr., 1971

Cohen, Miriam. *Will I Have A Friend?* Collier Books, 1967

Davis, Gibbs. *The Other Emily.* Houghton Mifflin, 1984

Delton, Judy. *Two Good Friends.* Crown, 1986

Graham, Bob. *Adventures of Charlotte and Henry.* Viking Kestrel, 1987

Heine, Helme. *Friends.* Macmillan, 1982

Hoff, Syd. *Who Will Be My Friend?* Harper & Row, 1960

Kellogg, Steven. *Best Friends.* Dial, 1986

Krauss, Ruth. *The Growing Story.* Harper & Row, 1947

Lobel, Arnold. *Frog and Toad.* Harper & Row, 1970

Mayer, Mercer. *All By Myself.* Golden Press, 1985

Mayer, Mercer. *When I Get Bigger.* Western, 1985

Parish, Peggy. *I Can - Can You?* Greenwillow, 1984

Prelutsky, Jack (selected by). *The Random House Book of Poetry for Children.* Random House, 1983

Prelutsky, Jack (selected by). *Read-Aloud Rhymes for the Very Young.* Knopf, 1986

Sharmat, Marjorie. *I'm Terrific.* Holiday, 1977

Smith, Robert Paul. *When I Am Big.* Harper & Row, 1965

Stren, Patti. *Hug Me.* Fitzhenry, 1984

Taylor, Barbara. *I Climb Mountains.* Women's Press, 1975

Williams, Sarah. *Round and Round The Garden.* Oxford

Wright, Betty Ren. *I Want To Read!* Golden Press, 1970

Zolotow, Charlotte. *The New Friend.* Crowell Jr., 1981

Records and Tapes

Bennett, Glenn. *I Must Be Growing.* Magic Dragon "I'm Just Me" "Brussell Sprouts" "Friend Of Mine" "I Must Be Growing" "Friends"

Disney Cassettes. *Silly Songs.* The Walt Disney Co., 1988, "What's Your Name?"

Johnstone, Ian. *Love And Warm Fuzzies.* Dandelion "Singing, Laughing...." "I Can Fly" "I Believe In Me" "Growing Up"

McGrath, Bob. *Songs & Games for Toddlers.* "I Want To Do It Myself" "Tommy Thumbs Up"

Millang, Steve. *We All Live Together Vol. 3.* Youngheart Records, 1979 "Simon Says"

Millang, Steve. *We All Live Together Vol. 4.* Youngheart Records, 1980 "Just Like Me"

Penner, Fred. *The Cat Came Back.* Troubadour Records, 1980 "Sandwiches"

Raffi. *Singable Songs for the Very Young.* Troubadour Records, 1976 "Brush Your Teeth" "I Wonder If I'm Growing" "The Sharing Song"

Rosenshontz. *Share It!* Kids' Records, 1982 "Eat It Up!"

Thomas, Marlo. *Free To Be...A Family.* A & M Records "Yourself Belongs To You" "Crowded Tub"